# Penguins

## A Compare and Contrast Book

by Cher Vatalaro

Only five of the 18 penguin species live in the cold Antarctic region. Yes, that means most penguins live in warm climates!

The Galapagos penguins even live just north and south of the equator! All other penguins only live in the Southern Hemisphere.

Unlike most birds, penguins don't fly through the air. Instead of wings, they use flippers to "fly" through the water.

Penguins waddle, hop, and slide on land.

When on land, most penguins live in groups called colonies. Some, like the yellow-eyed penguins live alone in forests.

Even though penguins mostly live in water, they lay eggs on land. Some hold their eggs on their feet to keep the eggs warm. Others create nests in rocks, sand, and crevices.

How else are they alike but different?

Adélie penguins have dark, black heads with white rings around their eyes.

African penguins have a thick black stripe and dots across their chest. They have pink patches of skin above their eyes that allow them to shed heat.

Chinstraps get their name after the stripe of black feathers on their "chin."

Emperors have yellow patches on the sides of their heads and orange stripes on their bottom beaks.

Erect-crested penguins
have yellow feathers
over their eyes that
they can make stand up
straight. Their beaks are
brownish orange.

Fiordland penguins have bright yellow feather crests from their red beaks, up over their eyes towards the back of their heads.

Galapagos penguins have a band of white that goes around their eyes down to their necks. They have a black band and dots across their chests.

Gentoo penguins have white wedges around their eyes and bright red spots on the sides of their beaks.

Humboldts have horseshoe-shaped white stripes that wrap around the sides of their heads. Like other "banded" penguins, they have a black stripe and dots across their chests.

King penguins have bright orange and yellow patches on the sides of their heads and on their chests. They have orange spots on their lower beaks. These penguins are sometimes confused with Emperor penguins.

Little penguins are
more blue and white
than black and white.

Macaroni penguins have bright yellow feather crests, a red beak, and red eyes. They have black throats.

Magellanic penguins have thick wide half-circles of white feathers from over their eyes around to their chins.

Like African penguins, they have pink, featherless areas on their faces and a black stripe across their chests.

Northern Rockhoppers have bright red eyes, orange-red beaks, and long yellow and black head feathers.

Royal penguins have gold and orange feathers on their heads and dark, red eyes. They have grey or white throats.

Snares penguins have yellow "eyebrow" feathers above their eyes.

Southern rockhoppers
have tufts of gold-
colored crest feathers
above their eyes.

Yellow-eyed penguins really do have yellow eyes. The tops of their heads are also covered in yellow feathers.

# For Creative Minds

## Penguin Fun Facts

Some birds, including some penguins, have feather tufts, called crests, on the top of their heads. Birds can usually control their crest feathers by raising or lowering them. Male birds might do this to attract females. They might do it to "talk" to other birds or to show they are scared. Erect-crested, royal, macaroni, northern rockhopper, southern rockhopper, Fiordland, Snares, and yellow-eyed penguins are considered "crested penguins."

Because African penguins make a braying sound like a donkey, they are sometimes called "jackass" penguins.

Just like we can be identified by fingerprints, we can identify individual banded penguins (African, Magellanic, Humboldt, and Galapagos) by the black spots on their chests.

Emperor penguins are the tallest penguins and can be as tall as 4 feet (1.2 meters). *How tall are you?*

The little penguin is the smallest species standing at just under 1 foot tall (30 cm).

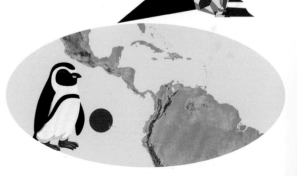

It's true... not all penguins live in the cold, polar region of Antarctica.

Except for Galapagos penguins that live on both sides of the equator, all other penguins live in the southern hemisphere. You will never find polar bears and penguins living together in the wild.

# Penguin Identification

Can you use the information in the book to identify these penguins?

How are beak shapes and colors alike or different? Describe eye colors and feathered head crests. Which ones look more alike than others?

1: yellow-eyed, 2: chinstrap. 3: emperor. 4: macaroni. 5; northern rockhopper. 6: African. 7: king. 8: royal. 9: Magellanic

# Where in the World?

Match the penguin-identifying color to see the approximate area where they live.

Galapagos

Little

Yellow-eyed

Fiordland

Erect-Crested

Royal

Chinstrap

Gentoo

King

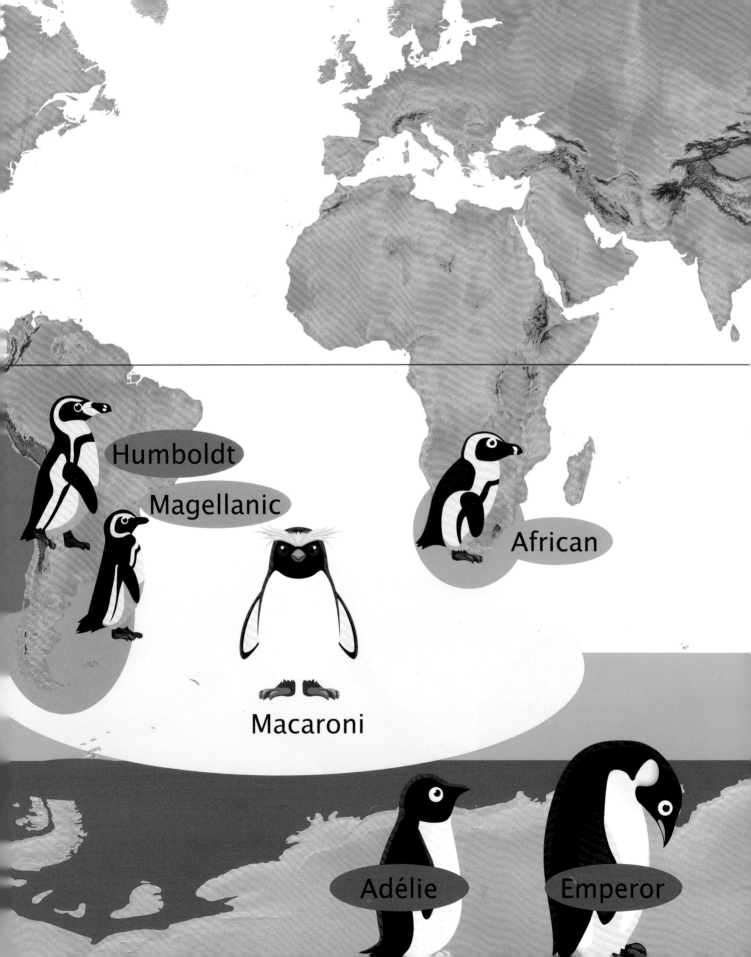

Humboldt

Magellanic

African

Macaroni

Adélie

Emperor

# Match the Adaptations

All living things have adaptations that help them survive in their habitats. Match the penguin adaptations.

**A** Penguins have amazing **beaks**. The tips of the beaks on some penguins have a hook on them to help grab fish. The inside of their mouths and tongues have small finger-like projections (papillae) to help the birds to swallow fish whole.

**B** Since penguins can't fly, their **wings (flippers)** are perfectly adapted for swimming. Their wings are hard and narrow like paddles to help move through the water.

**C** Like ducks, penguins have **webbed feet**. They use their feet for steering and braking in the water. Their nails help them climb and hop around on land.

Their feet are set back far on their bodies. That helps them swim but also makes them waddle on land.

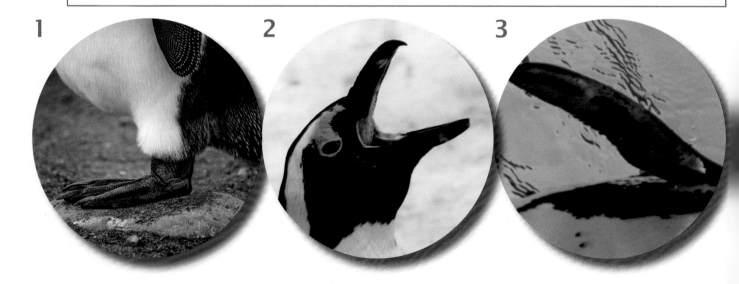

1        2        3

Answers: A2-beaks, B3-flippers, C1-webbed feet

Penguins can have up to 100 feathers per square inch on their bodies! They have more feathers than any other bird!

*Can you put 100 dots into a square inch?*

one
square
inch

**D**

Penguins have two kinds of **feathers**. They have an under layer that is made up of down feathers. This layer acts like a blanket and keeps the birds warm. The outer layer acts like a wet suit and helps to keep them dry. The outer feathers are oily which is what makes them waterproof.

**E**

Since penguins don't fly, they have no need for hollow **bones**, like most other birds. Instead, they have solid bones, just like humans!

Penguin **knees** are very high on their legs, very close to their "hips." Their knees are covered by skin and feathers so it is like when women wear tight skirts. Penguins have to take short steps because of their "tight skirts."

**F**

**Countershading** is a special type of camouflage used by many animals. Dark backs help them blend in with the dark ocean when seen from above. Their white bellies help them blend in with the lighter surface of the water when seen from below.

*What other animals can you think of that have countershading?*

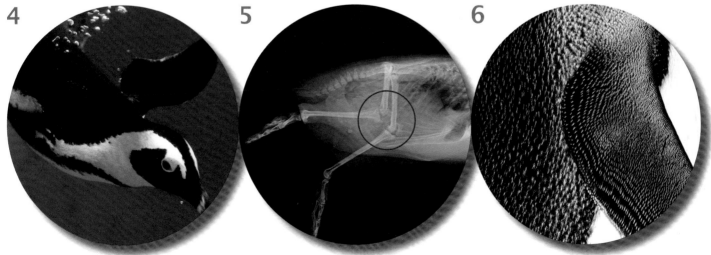

4        5        6

Answers: D6-feathers, E5-bones/knees, F4-countershading

Thanks to P. Dee Boersma, Professor of Conservation Biology, Evolution and Systematics at the University of Washington, Director of the Center for Ecosystem Sentinels and Co-Chair of the International Union for the Conservation of Nature SSC Penguin Specialist Group for verifying the information in this book.

Thanks to the Mystic Aquarium for the use of their x-ray photos of penguin bones and knees. All other photographs are licensed through Adobe Stock Photos or Shutterstock.

Library of Congress Cataloging-in-Publication Data

Names: Vatalaro, Cher, 1988- author.
Title: Penguins : a compare and contrast book / by Cher Vatalaro.
Description: Mt. Pleasant : Arbordale Publishing, LLC, [2021] | Includes
    bibliographical references.
Identifiers: LCCN 2021013707 (print) | LCCN 2021013708 (ebook) | ISBN
    9781643519876 (paperback) | ISBN 9781638170259 (adobe pdf) | ISBN
    9781638170440 (epub) | ISBN 9781638170068 (Interactive, dual-language,
    read-aloud ebook)
Subjects: LCSH: Penguins--Juvenile literature.
Classification: LCC QL696.S473 V35 2021  (print) | LCC QL696.S473  (ebook)
    | DDC 598.47--dc23
LC record available at https://lccn.loc.gov/2021013707
LC ebook record available at https://lccn.loc.gov/2021013708

Bibliography/ Bibliografía:
"All about Penguins - Conservation & Research | SeaWorld Parks & Entertainment." Seaworld.org, 2010, seaworld.org/
    animals/all-about/penguins/conservation-and-research/.
"Aptenodytes Patagonicus (King Penguin)." Animal Diversity Web, 2010, animaldiversity.org/accounts/Aptenodytes_
    patagonicus/.
Bellows, Nick. "Eudyptes Robustus (Snares Penguin)." Animal Diversity Web, animaldiversity.org/accounts/Eudyptes_robustus/.
"Bird Crests Are More than Just Ornaments." The Spruce, www.thespruce.com/meaning-of-crest-385208.
Braswell, Tricia. "Eudyptes Pachyrhynchus (Fiordland Penguin)." Animal Diversity Web, animaldiversity.org/accounts/
    Eudyptes_pachyrhynchus/.
Burchman, Jenny. "Eudyptes Sclateri (Erect-Crested Penguin)." Animal Diversity Web, animaldiversity.org/accounts/
    Eudyptes_sclateri/.
"Can You Name All the Penguin Species?" The Spruce, www.thespruce.com/penguin-species-list-385429.
Combos, Veronica. "Pygoscelis Adeliae (Adélie Penguin)." Animal Diversity
"Eudyptes Chrysocome (Rockhopper Penguin)." Animal Diversity Web, 2019, animaldiversity.org/accounts/Eudyptes_
    chrysocome/.
"Every Penguin, Ranked: Which Species Are We Most at Risk of Losing?" BirdLife, 2017, www.birdlife.org/list-penguin-species.
"Global Penguin Society." Www.globalpenguinsociety.org, www.globalpenguinsociety.org/index.html#species.
Howard, Laura. "Sphenisciformes (Penguins)." Animal Diversity Web, animaldiversity.org/accounts/Sphenisciformes/.
Newtoff, Kiersten. "Pygoscelis Papua (Gentoo Penguin)." Animal Diversity Web, animaldiversity.org/accounts/Pygoscelis_papua/.
Nissley, Heidi. "Spheniscus Humboldti (Humboldt Penguin)." Animal Diversity Web, animaldiversity.org/accounts/
    Spheniscus_humboldti/.
"Penguin | Species | WWF." World Wildlife Fund, 2019, www.worldwildlife.org.
"Static Map of the Geographical Distribution of Penguins." PenguinWorld, www.penguinworld.com/map/staticmap.html.
Reynolds, Katie. "Eudyptes Chrysolophus (Macaroni Penguin)." Animal Diversity Web, animaldiversity.org/accounts/
    Eudyptes_chrysolophus/.
Wahlstrom, Joshua. "Spheniscus Mendiculus (Galapagos Penguin)." Animal Diversity Web, animaldiversity.org/accounts/
    Spheniscus_mendiculus/.
Williams, Tony D (1995). *The Penguins.* Oxford, England: Oxford University Press.
Wit, Kirsty de. "Eudyptes Schlegeli (Royal Penguin)." Animal Diversity Web, animaldiversity.org/accounts/Eudyptes_schlegeli/.

Lexile Level: 890L

Text Copyright 2021 © by Cher Vataloro

Printed in the US
This product conforms to CPSIA 2008
First Printing

Arbordale Publishing, LLC
Mt. Pleasant, SC 29464
www.ArbordalePublishing.com